Celebrate Mardi Gras Adult Coloring Books

COLORING BOOK WITH CARNIVAL AND VENETIAN MASK ART DRAWINGS

Adam and Marky™

Ginzburg Press

Adam and Marky™/Ginzburg Press
www.ginzburgpress.com

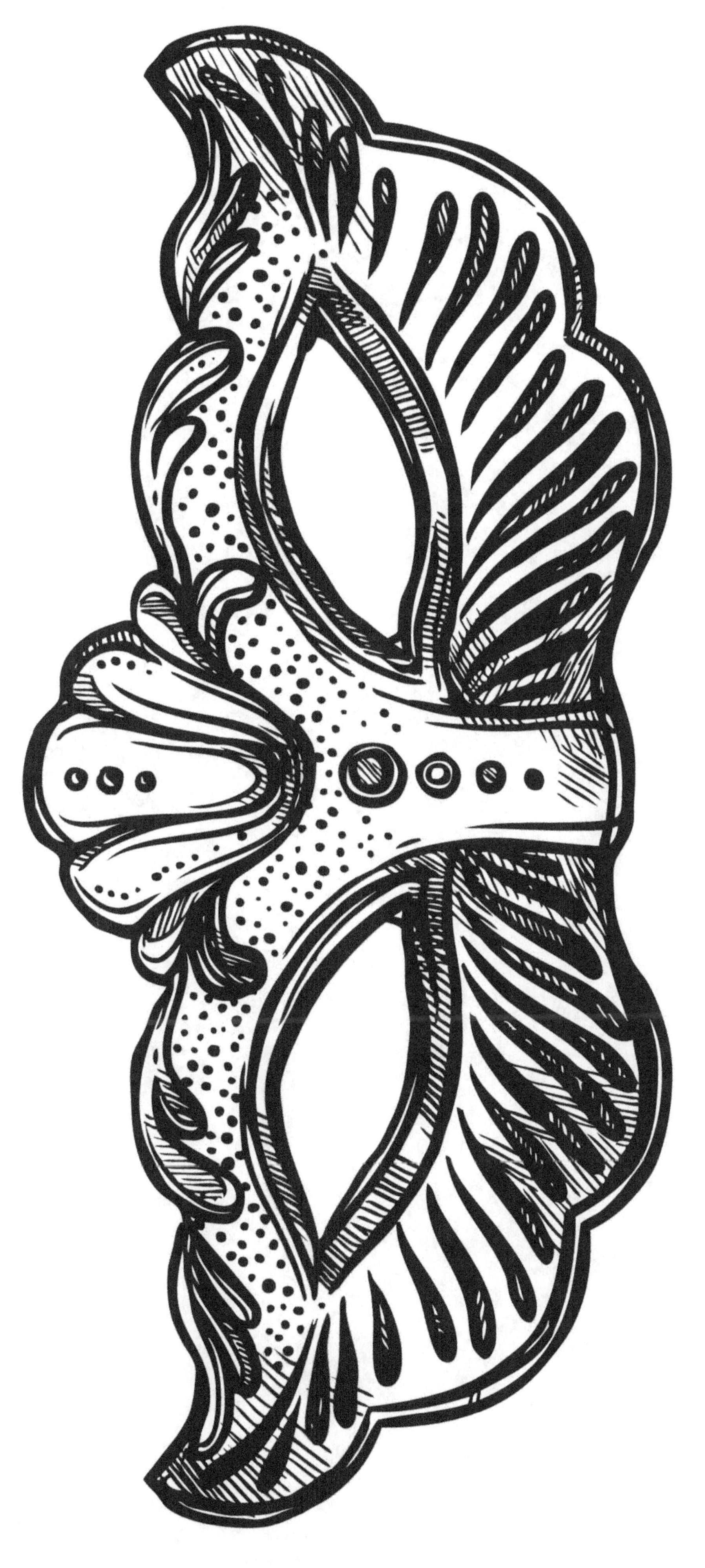

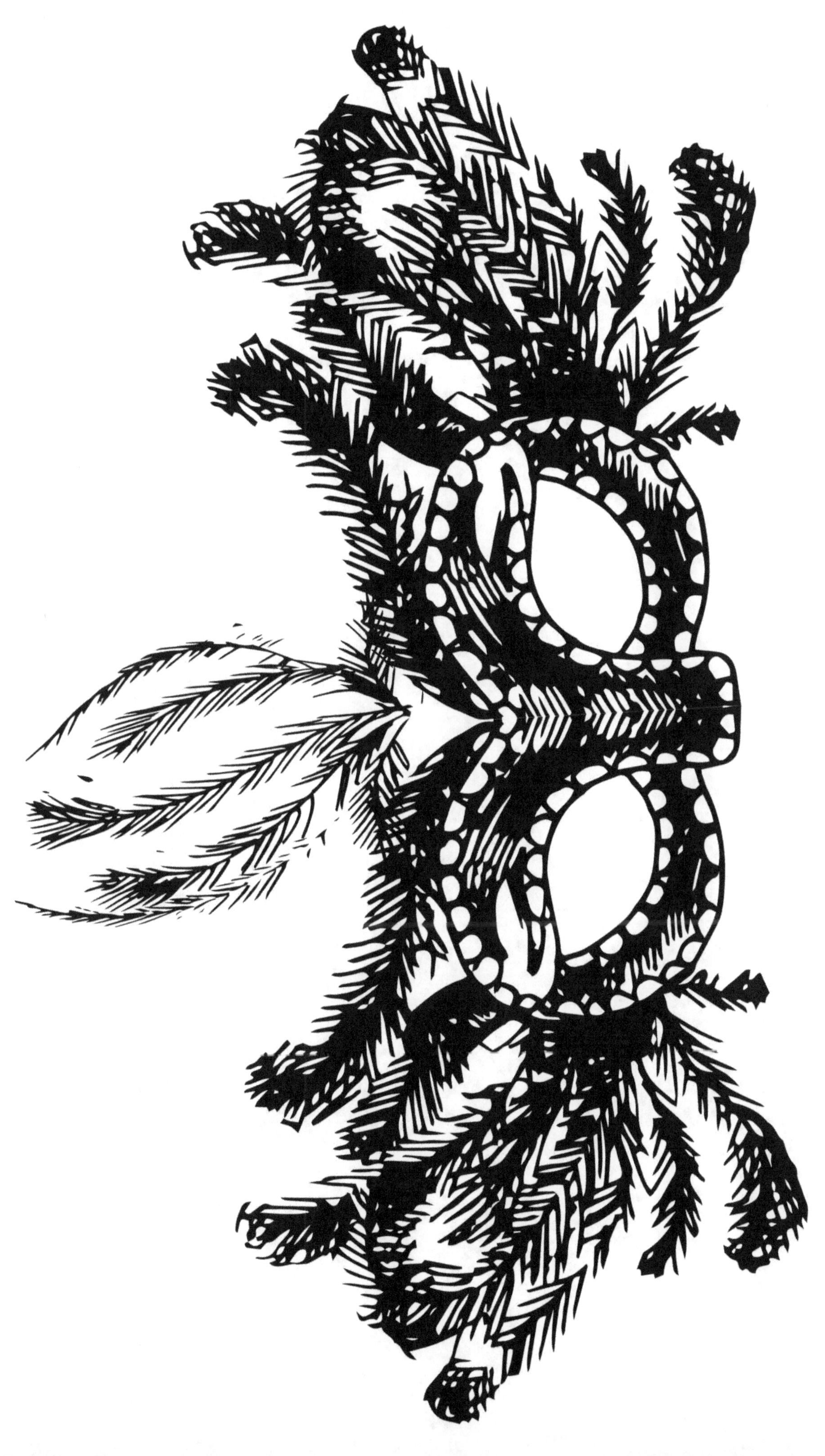

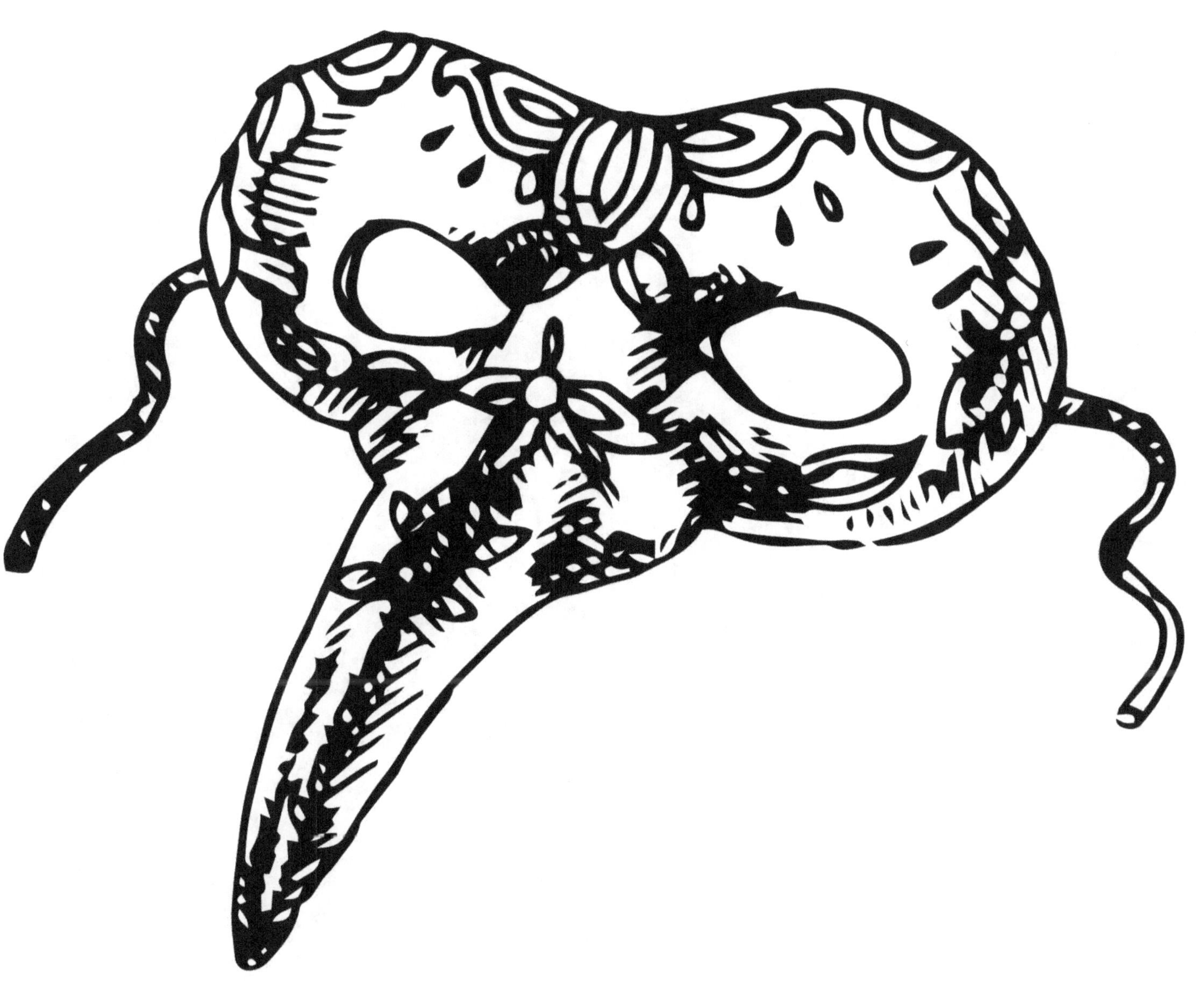

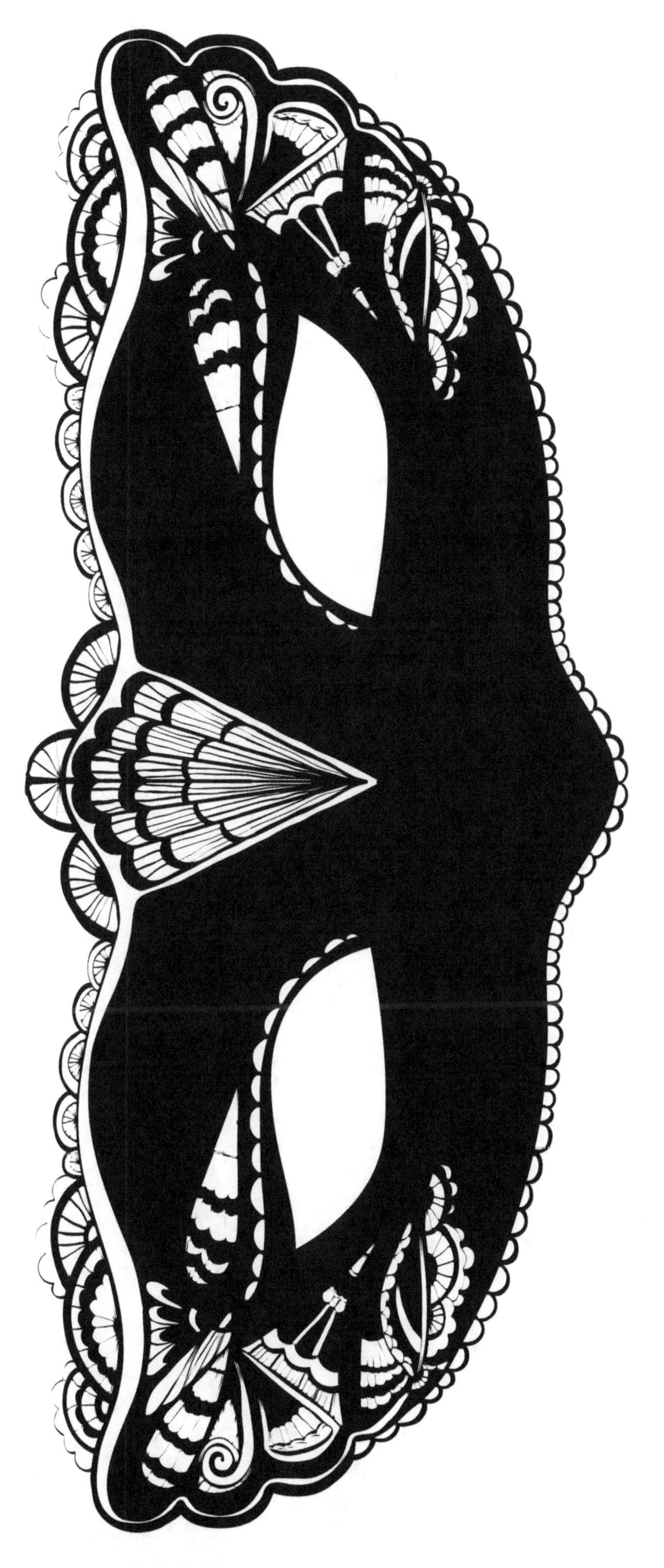

The Adam and Marky™ brand is brought to you by Ginzburg Press. Ginzburg Press is a digital production company that distributes merchandise, books, apparel and animated short films.

Follow us on

Facebook: https://www.facebook.com/adamandmarky
Twitter: https://twitter.com/ginzburgpress
Instagram: https://www.instagram.com/adamandmarky/
Website: https://adamandmarky.com/
Etsy Store: https://adamandmarky.etsy.com
YouTube: https://www.youtube.com/ginzburgpress
Amazon Store:
https://www.amazon.com/stores/page/E9332374-4D5E-4744-9DA5-E5DD985F8B2C
Merchandise, Apparel, Books and Movies on Amazon:
https://www.amazon.com/shop/influencer-2d0150db
Adam and Marky Author Page: https://amazon.com/author/adamandmarky

www.ingramcontent.com/pod-product-compliance
Lightning Source LLC
Chambersburg PA
CBHW081632250726
48657CB00009B/2845